ISBN-13: 9798584473457
ISBN-10: 1477123456

Cover design by: Canva
Library of Congress Control Number: 2018675309
Printed in the United States of America

# THE LEADERS OF PROGRESS

## 10 Inspiring Stories of Overcoming Struggles During a Global Pandemic

### Juliette M. Bruner

*For my parents and mentors, thank you for your support and for helping me become the woman I am today.*

*"Without progress the world will never move forward."*

# CONTENTS

# INTRODUCTION

In March 2020, a global pandemic struck the world and caused a massive shutdown. COVID-19 resulted in a significant amount of job loss across the globe. I was curious about the impacts on different industries and how professionals could combat the obstacles that ensued from this universal struggle. *The Leaders of Progress* dives into each of the individual stories of struggles or events during the pandemic. The experts interviewed discussed their philosophies in the workforce, strategies to combat obstacles, and provided advice to future generations. The industries examined include live entertainment, energy, activism, politics, law, marketing, real estate, and exercise.

Specifically, after conducting research, the Live Entertainment industry seems to be predominantly impacted through a labor focus due to in-person activities' limitations. We saw a similar decrease in real estate employment; however, significant recovery occured near the end of 2020. Through the political and marketing lens, there was a substantial increase in opportunity and community development. The oil and gas industry suffered many downfalls due to the lack of travel, decrease in demand for the commodity and gasoline usage; however, due to its status as an essential industry, the government never shut down production. Thus, there were less job losses than expected in the oil gas and other energy sectors. Through activism and Yoga, we saw a rise in individuals engaged with others over virtual communication such as zoom and Microsoft teams. Furthermore, it's fascinating to witness how many people have relied upon and supported each other during these troublesome times.

At the beginning of the pandemic, I founded the publication Ression Magazine to highlight progress worldwide. Our goal is to unite people from various backgrounds and perspectives to highlight positivity and innovation. We primarily focus on subject areas pertaining to Sports, Beauty, Politics, Entertainment, Study, Wellness, and Business. We published our first issue in June 2020 and had our official launch in May 2020. Ression Magazine strives to inspire individuals to continue to progress in their lives. I am so grateful for every individual who graciously set aside time to provide interviews for Ression Magazine and

The Leaders of Progress. The conversations we shared were truly inspiring and I believe will spark motivation in many individuals.

# TEN QUESTIONS WITH PRESIDENT AND CEO OF ENTERTAINMENT BENEFITS GROUP, BRETT REIZEN

B rett D. Reizen attended the University of Miami, where he received a Bachelor's Degree in Business Administration. Before his founding and leadership of Entertainment Benefits Group, Reizen was Senior Business Development Manager for EnSpot.com. EnSpot.com is a marketing company that managed advertisements for movie studios, concert tours, Broadway shows, and entertainment venues.

Reizen is currently the President and Chief Executive Officer of Entertainment Benefits Group (EBG). Brett Reizen was the co-founder of the company in 2001 with a vision to provide exclusive access to benefits, discounts, or special offers in recreational experiences to individuals through its program TicketsatWork. After the events of September 11, 2001, Reizen wanted to uplift individuals to help morale in the workplace. Through TicketsatWork, Reizen has provided excellent customer service and marketing that 15 years later made TicketsatWork a household name. TicketsatWork was later featured on Fortune Magazine's "100 Best Companies to Work For."

Reizen led this innovative movement that connected the world's greatest travel entertainment brands to companies and businesses globally. These opportunities include unlimited access to theme parks, Broadway and Vegas shows, major sporting events, concerts, tours, attractions, hotels, rental cars, retail gift cards, and other luxuries. Under his leadership, he grew the company from a small tech start-up to one of the largest organizations for travel and entertainment in the United States. Reizen utilized and managed programs that were essential to the growth of EBG. EBG developed into one of the most extensive corporate benefits programs in the United

States of America. EBG provides members of corporations exclusive access to products from the world's top travel and entertainment brands. EBG has reportedly created client relationships with more than 40,000 corporations and over 50 million employees nationwide.

**What is your career, and what is your day to day?**

I founded the Entertainment Benefits group on September 12, 2001. We are an eCommerce business, and we specialize in travel entertainment. We transact a high volume of sales and travel through multiple different just distribution channels. Corporate benefits is our largest channel; we reach about 59,000 employees through over 40,000 corporate clients through a corporate perks program. Our clients' employees enter with access to unique offers not available to the public, for example, theme parks, attractions, Broadway shows, Vegas hotels, rental cars, movies, and theater. We also provide various other non-travel and attendant products like cars, electronics, flowers, and a lot of different unique offers that you have access to because you work for a corporation. We also have some other technology platforms that we provide for distribution partners. We power the whole website for AAA, which has about 42 million members, and Sam's Club with approximately 45 million members. We have many other different partners like that are eCommerce and all digital;

3

we manage their platform for them.

**What is your philosophy in your work?**

Our business has been a high growth business and has had a lot of ambition since I started the company. I grew it into a large organization of great shareholders and very supportive board of directors. Our goal has been to be a leader in the industries we operate in, and we have been very successful in many ways. We are the largest seller of our product for many of our partners, including major theme parks and attractions, the biggest Broadway shows, and hotels. What drives me is continuous growth for our organization and the executives and the team members working for us. They always want to keep growing stronger and better.

**How has COVID-19 affected your work?**

Well, being in the travel entertainment business, it's had an enormous impact. We went from having 600 employees to about just over 200. So, it's been a challenging period because we have lost many committed, loyal, dedicated team members, which was frustrating for many reasons. I can tell you our executive teams, leadership teams, and the entire team that we still have behind us is committed, and it has been such an incredible thing to see how people have come together, doing more with less. Coming out of this, we will be stronger; we're going to be better; we'll be wiser. Hopefully, we will be able to hire many of the people we had to let go of. I'm not sure if it will be six months from now or 12 months, hopefully not much longer than that.

I think 2022 and 2023 are going to be probably the best years of our business. Specifically, from a live entertainment standpoint, theme parks, attractions, and people just wanting to go out, spend money, and have a good time. We have access to such a large, closed loop audience, and such a loyal audience, for accessing these products and services through us and their employer. We've got a pretty bright future in front of us. We have to be patient with it; a lot of people are suffering. Our employees, many of them are accepting reduced pay. California is entirely closed, and that's a large part of my business. Vegas is now completely closed; Broadway has been closed since March. It's taken a significant toll on our financials as an organization and mental stability, but we have just had to lean on each other and work digitally. We had never been remote, so we have had to adapt, change our call centers, and change our technology teams. We went from operating as a business with offices in multiple cities to every other office being remote. I think we all realized how much we enjoyed traveling, being in front of each other, and doing in-person meetings, versus doing everything at home over the phone.

**How are you able to overcome struggles caused by the COVID-19 pandemic?**

The beginning was challenging, we were staring down millions and millions of dollars in customer refunds, but our supplier partners have been extremely pro partner and great partners for us. We have put together new policies and new technologies to ease everyone's burden and try to make it as customer-friendly as possible with cancellation refund changes. But it was very challenging. We just had to work together to keep a positive mindset and continuously remind each other that we have to stay positive. We have everybody committed to our leadership project teams. Being positive is the only way to get through an issue. I think we have all been able to appreciate people we work with, and positive energy is something that I have preached for a long time within the business, and if you don't have it, we don't want you working for us. It's super important to make sure that you don't have too many mental and physical stresses in your life and understand how the business can be supportive for you personally and professionally. I think getting exercise, eating right, and continuously preaching positivity to our different management departments. We can all support each other during this time.

**How have you're marketing or business strategies been changed or influenced by the COVID-19 pandemic?**

We have had to reduce our sales teams, eliminate a lot of our advertising spending, and adopt new strategies that we've applied to in-person marketing initiatives. It's changed quite a bit. In the last couple of months, starting in November, we have built up a little bit of a sales team and began to be an aggressive side again. We have slowly grown back and been on the offensive to come out of the stabilization phase and start acquiring new business. We also want to start companies that are just trying to hold on, especially in healthcare and finance. They're so busy that the very last thing they want to do is mess with soft and voluntary benefits for employees. However, they do want to make things better for employees, so we're trying to take our shots when we have to be smart about it.

**Since California and Nevada are closed, has your company been focusing on Florida since Disney World and other attractions are open?**

We have been fortunate that Disney and Universal have always been in the top two partners that we've had across the board. We exclusively run the corporate program for Universal Orlando. They have been one of our closest partners since inception for many years. We are very strategic with them with all their marketing strategies, and it hasn't changed. It hasn't missed a beat. But I think we are fortunate we have good weather in Florida, and the parks are open; they have done a great job keeping things safe. As a result, people have grown their confidence to go to these attractions during COVID.

It started about 20% capacity, then they increased to 25% and then now it's a 35% as of even a few days ago. The next step is for government officials to decrease the social distancing range from 10 feet to 6 feet because it looks like it's busier than it is since the lines are so spaced out. I think the purpose is to continuously try to get more people in and make sure it's safe. We're not only focusing on Orlando but every warm environment, beach getaways are very popular, especially now. Not just the Orlando parks but attraction areas where people can spend time outside and have family gatherings.

**As a whole, the entertainment industry has been impacted by the pandemic; from your perspective or knowledge, could you explain the specifics of the impacts the entertainment industry has faced?**

Well, that depends on what type of entertainment, for example, sporting events and concerts have no live attendance. Revenue has come to a halt; specifically, Cirque de Soleil filed for bankruptcy protection; however, they already had a lot of debt on the books. It's been a considerable impact on a lot of other organizations in entertainment. Theaters, such as AMC and Regal, are basically closed because they don't have enough products to sell, and people are uncomfortable going to theaters. It's been challenging.

The Broadway community is the shows' producers, all the stagehands, the actors, the ushers in the box, office personnel, and everybody. There are many people involved in each production, and they're all not making any money. It's had a massive impact across the board for everybody in live entertainment, whether in Broadway, touring, Vegas, or live music. The concert industry is basically at a halt. So hopefully, everyone involved in the industry can get back to normal quickly.

**What advice do you have for teenagers preparing for their future careers?**

Well, I didn't know what I wanted to do. So that was my challenge. I just knew I wanted to get into business. I wanted to make an impact on a lot of people, and I wanted to make a lot of money. That's what I wanted to do. So, I would say first, find your passion. Think about what you like to do; you have to enjoy it. Whatever work you do, you should figure out what you enjoy because people that go to work every day are just going to collect a paycheck. Number one, it's not good for your mental health to do that. It's also not good for your employer because you're not getting the most out of your work if you're not really into it. I think you have to find out what you want to do and love it.

Second, set some goals for yourself and keep increasing those goals. Make them realistic but reach each goal. Have a stretch goal, a goal you want to achieve in a year or two, keep raising the bar, and then work your ass off. I think the challenge with teenagers and millennials is too many people are entitled and don't have the same work ethic. A lot of people still do, but a lot of people don't. What's important is that those who put in the extra time, energy, and effort are the people who get ahead. There are those people who get jobs when there are limited jobs out there. Because people that sit around and say, there are no jobs. That's not true. There are always jobs. Find them! You have to be very persistent and creative to talk to a manager, get an interview to explain why they should hire you, and have confidence in yourself. Make sure you're well versed, do your preparation, and whatever you're doing, have faith in yourself. That's super important. Once you have that ingredient, you can take on the world.

I think, especially when you're young, you have so many opportunities. It doesn't matter how old you are; if you're super young, you still have unique opportunities to grow fast within organizations. When I started the business, I had a babyface. I was often not taken seriously, and it wasn't easy. When I was 25, I had to manage 45, or 55, or 60-year-olds. It was strange; it was awkward. But as time went on, it got less awkward; soon, more young leaders were out there. Young people are running organizations and businesses now. There are 25 to 30-year-old very successful CEOs, even coaches of major sporting teams. So, I think age is not a factor as much as experience, intelligence, confidence, knowledge. All that's important is hard work, so if you have all that, you can do anything.

**Can you provide an example of a specific situation that COVID impacted a project and how you were able to find a solution to overcome it?**

I would say there are too many to name. When COVID first happened, I was on the phone every day, seven days a week from 7:30 in the morning until 11:30 pm or midnight. I would be talking with my finance teams, private equity partners, and shareholders, changing policies, technology, structure, reporting, looking at cash flow, and analyzing everything. So, there are too many times to share individual examples of making quick decisions because we had to make decisions quickly to survive. We made all of those decisions in the early days. The first two or three weeks of this have allowed us to get back into the business to last 12 months. Since then, we've managed the cash flow very effectively because the number one thing is longevity to survive the crisis. We don't know what's ahead of us in the next two months, three months, or six months. So, we have to be conservative, but we have to do as much as possible for our employees. Also, staying balanced and ensuring that the company can sit around and survive well while doing everything we possibly can for our employees.

**What advice would you give teenagers that are having difficulties discovering what career they would like to pursue? What advice would you give someone aspiring for your career?**

With COVID, it isn't easy because I think you need to be in offices, have a real-world experience, and be on the phone with people to create relationships. You can understand if you like something or don't like it, so you can pivot and try different experiences. But try to think about other ways and live through it, talk it through. Don't be afraid to ask questions until you're rude about it. You could change your questions' framework and design if you didn't like the answer you got or didn't understand it. Then as far as my career, I'd say I am in multiple industries.

But if you bring them all together, I am more about digital marketing and eCommerce. I think technology is going to take even more and more power. Across the board and all industries are getting more and more critical. Things are being digitized, manual labor and labor will be taken over by automation as much as possible and AI. I think any career I would suggest should understand technology, digital, online marketing, and the digital space. There are many different digital marketing courses if you like marketing and making things happen. I think there's a lot of opportunities for people to get involved. It doesn't matter the industry with digital marketing; you could sell toilets, travel entertainment, market flowers, or dog toys, digital marketing is all the same. It's understanding all the nature and details that go behind it. So, there's a shortage of players. There's an excellent opportunity for young and upcoming talent to create a promising career in any space. So, in this space, there are opportunities to learn how to take advantage of them.

# TEN QUESTIONS WITH BISON OIL & GAS, I, II, AND III, LLC, CEO J. AUSTIN AKERS

John "Austin" Akers is a Denver, Colorado native. At the age of 15, he founded his first business doing land work for a family friend in the oil and gas sector. By the time Akers was 16, he bought and sold leases throughout the Rocky Mountains, Wyoming, Colorado, and Montana as a Landman for Contex Energy Company, LLC, and founding Buffalo Royalties, LLC.

Akers attended the School of Industrial and Labor

Relations at Cornell University. Towards the end of his college years, when Akers was a junior at Cornell University, the financial crash of 2008 occurred. Akers had made significant connections as an independent oil and gas landman. He utilized those connections from his prior years of work in the industry to find opportunities in the energy sector. During his senior year at Cornell, he started a mineral buying brokerage company to sell mineral rights.

After college, Akers relocated to Houston, Texas, and continued his mineral business, which continued to thrive. He was offered an opportunity to work as a landman at Linn Energy, Inc. During his employment with Linn Energy, the business developed into a $10 Billion company, and his job experience grew. In 2012, Akers joined forces with his current partner, and they formed Logos Resources, LLC. The company was backed by LOGOS Capital Management and Arclight Capital Partners and had assets in the San Juan Basin, which they later sold in 2014. In 2015, Akers and his partner founded Bison Oil & Gas I, LLC. Bison is a private equity-backed company, and it has grown to Bison Oil & Gas II, LLC, and Bison Oil & Gas, III, LLC. He is currently Bison's Chief Executive Officer.

**What is your career and day-to-day?**

I'm the CEO at Bison Oil & Gas. My day-to-day consists

of many things; no two days are the same. I do a lot of communication and strategic planning with our financial backers with a company called Carnelian Energy Capital. I'm in touch with them almost daily, trying to work on plans about how much we want to drill if we're going to make acquisitions, if we're going to sell assets, and we discuss certain personnel decisions. So that's probably one large part of my job. The second large part of my job is communicating with all the employees here about our goals, how to achieve them, and letting them do their work to hit our goals. I have many discussions with our land, regulatory, and human resources departments and our finance and accounting groups. Then probably the third part is making analytical decisions on our strategies. The final part is working on deals or negotiating purchase and sale agreements or dealing with landowners, which's become a smaller part, but it's still definitely a part.

**What is your philosophy in your work?**

I think we've tried to create a culture of enjoying work and having clear, concise goals that people can look to achieve. Then, at the same time, trying to promote a culture of being good humans. So really, to round that out, we give people many latitudes to do what they do well. We hire only the best, at least we try to hire only the best, and we're usually successful. We try to let those people use their skills and try not to get into their business but try to provide them with a company that supports them, has a good culture, and has very clear goals that they can look to achieve.

**Have political issues surrounding the oil and gas industry changed or remained constant because of the COVID-19 pandemic towards the oil and gas industry, or has it stayed pretty consistent?**

I don't think COVID has changed the perception of the oil and gas industry in politics. I think the only thing it's done is been a boom to democratic candidates in that respect. Now that they're in power, it's going to be difficult for us [in the oil and gas industry]. But I don't think COVID-19 had a direct impact on us, more of an indirect.

**How has COVID-19 affected or impacted your company's work?**

In the oil and gas business, probably more so than most other businesses, there's a ton of teamwork because it's such a complex industry. I mean, I would argue it's one of the most complex industries, you're matching people, from scientists, engineers, business people, finance people, and politicians, there's just a million variables to every day. We do many team meetings, and being in-person in those team meetings, I can tell you, it is a lot more effect-ive than being on zoom or teams and trying to do team meetings. We've gotten by and learned a lot about remote work and how it can, in some circumstances, be more efficient or more productive. I would say on the whole, particularly when it comes to sort of the higher-level employees. They are making some very consequential and important decisions that need to communicate with everyone. It's been tough. We've got better at it as time has gone on, but I would be lying if I said, I think we're going to remote work for the rest of our lives. We're not.

**How were you able to overcome these struggles?**

I think in a lot of ways, you just had to let it go. I mean, it was something that we couldn't control, and you had to accept that. Then you had to try to make the best of the situation. Initially, we tried to push back against what eventually was apparent was an inevitable sort of transi-tion to remote work for at least a period. It wasn't helpful. If anything, it just caused more problems. So that was ac-cepting the situation and trying to make the best out of it, and looking at how we could still enhance communica-tion, even if it had to be remote.

**How has your business strategy been changed or influ-enced by the COVID-19 pandemic?**

I think it's been influenced in that certain people can work remotely. I would say that's a minority of our company, but we probably have 10% to 20% of our employees who can work remotely without any negative effects. In some cases, people have had a positive influence on their work efficiencies and happiness as employees, which tends to make people work better. I think we're looking at embracing that for the small number of folks that this will work for. Regarding our overall business strategies, I think it's clear that a strategy we had already used pretty extensively, which is hedging, to account for potential risk, and commodity presence was essential. We'll probably have done more hedging than we used to do, even though we used to do a lot. I think the other thing is perhaps just proven to us that in the oil and gas business for the last ten years or from probably call it 2010, through 2018, you could quickly build and sell companies, and I don't think that exists anymore. COVID has perhaps just exaggerated that effect now with lack of demand and many companies going bankrupt in the industry, just focusing on profitability instead of growth. So, it's again an indirect effect, not a specific effect from COVID. But definitely had an impact.

**Have your company's rigs been able to continue to operate during the pandemic or were you forced to shut down because of government action?**

No, we were never shut down. The oil and gas industry was always considered an essential business, in particular oil and gas operations. So, we have not had to shut down any of our active rigs or fracks, so that has not luckily been that horrible. We've been forced to shut down portions of the office. But in terms of necessary operations and people, we've mostly been able to keep going. It hasn't been as bad as we initially feared; it could have been better.

**Can you provide an example of a specific situation that COVID impacted a project and how you found a solution to overcome it?**

I mean, we've had important folks leading projects, even if they haven't gotten COVID, that might have been exposed as somebody who has gotten COVID, or something along those lines. It's impacted our ability to execute on the timelines we're trying to execute on. I think we've just had to get a lot more flexible with our ability to move those people out of the office quickly and move them online, but still make sure that they have access to all the team members they need to accomplish their projects. Technology has been a big thing in that regard, making sure that everyone has the appropriate cameras, microphones, and all these things that you never think you're going to have to worry about that much, and that becomes a huge deal. It's been crucial to have backup plans and comprehensive plans around COVID. For example, when we're drilling wells, we make sure our contractors have the policies and procedures they need in case somebody on a rig gets COVID. You can't move the drilling rig, and you don't want to stop because it will cost you about $50,000 a day to sit there and not do anything. The same thing applies to a frack fleet, working with our vendors to ensure that they have those procedures and policies in place to protect against shutdowns.

**The lack of travel has significantly impacted the oil and gas industry during the pandemic. How has Bison been able to overcome this obstacle?**

I mean, prices are down, so hedging has been a huge part of our ability to avoid the type of revenue decreases that many of our peers have seen. The other thing that Bison has done is gotten rid of our traditional debt structure. In the latter part of 2019, we went with a more second lien type of debt deal with very limited covenants in debt. By not having very strict covenants on our debt and hedging simultaneously, we haven't had a type of revenue or production reserve impacts that would cause us to be in default. We haven't had any issues with our debt providers, and that has been very positive. Finally, I think just where we are, we can drill profitable wells, even at pretty significantly low prices, like we can be profitable in the 30s [dollars per barrel of oil] if we have to, but we don't like drilling in the 30s. So, as a result, we haven't had to lay anyone off and deal with the type of debt issue that many other folks have. Those are probably the three things that enabled us to get through without too many problems.

**What advice do you have for teenagers and young adults preparing for their future careers? What advice would you give to someone aspiring for your career?**

I would make sure that they understand all forms of energy, not just oil and gas. I think if we're honest with ourselves, oil and gas, it's not dead by any means, but it's not going to grow at the same pace it has in the past, and in some ways, an industry in decline. Now, that doesn't mean you can't make good money and be successful. It's just that the opportunities as a whole are going to be smaller, and you're not going to have as much ability or running room. I think the running room in energy is in its alternatives or working with natural gas or things like that. The government's going to be spending trillions of dollars and themes on that stuff. So, I think there will be vast amounts of money and opportunity in the energy space as a whole. If there's one thing that's clear is that the need for energy is not going away. In fact, that need is increasing at a record pace, and it's not going to stop unless people decide they don't want to consume, which we all know is not going to happen anytime soon.

So, I would say that for someone looking to get into the energy business and lead an energy company, don't let salary dictate what job you choose. I know many people from college focused on getting an additional $5,000 or $10,000 in their salary and took menial positions, and they didn't grow in those jobs. If your focus is not to grow, and you want to get the best salary, then I guess that's fine. But I would say for people looking to grow in their careers, they should look for jobs that give you the ability to learn and grow. That would probably be my biggest piece of advice for people coming out of college or people coming out of high school even.

# TEN QUESTIONS WITH UNITED NATIONS SPEAKER, AMELIA MARCUM

P resident and one of the founders of the Girl Up Chapter at Regis Jesuit High School, Amelia Marcum, joined the Girl Up International Board. Marcum has collaborated with girls from ten different countries to advise Girl Up Organization and promote gender equality worldwide. Many of the jobs Marcum undertakes is leading the international summit.

Although many events that Marcum would

be organizing have been sadly canceled due to the coronavirus pandemic, she was one of the few selected to speak at the United Nations assembly. Marcum is delighted to use her platform as a female and native woman to speak out on society's injustices.

At the United Nations, she discussed the murders of indigenous women providing an example of a woman in her tribe. She continues by explaining the Savannah's Act that was recently passed by Congress and it's affect on her tribe. Savannah, the inspiration for the Savannah's Act, was a member of Marcum's tribe in North Dakota. Marcum explains how native women "are murdered at ten times the rate of the national average." She concludes that Congress passing this act was a "happy moment" for her because this is one step to combat this epidemic.

Marcum was frustrated by the lack of awareness this issue has been receiving and is excited to highlight this subject, providing it the attention it deserves. Although Marcum recognizes that there is still much work to be done, passing the Savannah's Act will not resolve this issue, but this is an important step. Amelia Marcum is an avid feminist and activist and will be attending Stanford University in the fall of 2021.

**How did you discover Girl up?**

I discovered Girl Up after attending the 2018 leadership summit in Washington DC. I was incredibly inspired by the empowering speakers, Teen Advisors, and attendees who were all doing such important work in their communities. When I got back home to Denver, I decided to start the very first Girl Up club at my school. Over the last three years we've hosted multiple events, speaking engagements, and valuable discussions. I am so grateful to have had the opportunity to work with Girl Up!

**Why did Girl Up become so important to you,
and what did you do with this motivation?**

I have always had proud feminist. I believe that no matter who you are, or where are you come from our identities are all equally valuable and it is important that we are given the opportunity to use our voices. At the leadership summit, I was given the opportunity to lobby for the Keeping Girls in School Act on Capitol Hill. I was incredibly empowered by the impact that I was able to have and wanted to do my part to help ensure that girls around the world were given the same opportunity as me. Girl Up has created so many amazing initiatives to help support young girls and I have worked with my club to participate in their programming as much as possible.

**How did you become a part of Girl Up international board?**

I applied to be a team advisor last spring. I remembered seeing all the innovative activities that Teen Advisors shared at the leadership summit and I wanted to have the chance to do the same for my own community. I could not be more honored to have been given this opportunity and continuing my involvement as a leader in the organization.

**What are some of your duties?**

As a Girl Up Teen advisor, my goal is to advance the Girl Up mission, provide feedback on key organization strategy, represent Girl Up at major events, and energize girls to take action around the world.

**How have the people you met through this position impacted your perspectives?**

My fellow teen advisers are some of the most inspiring girls that I have ever met in my life. The positivity that radiates around them somehow makes me even more grateful to be a part of this incredible organization. There are nine countries represented in a team advisor program, so our perspective is very global. I have learned so much about the different political systems, cultural norms, and public policies around the world. It has been especially eye-opening during the pandemic to understand the different approaches to health and safety throughout our world. I know I can count on these girls no matter what and I can't wait to spend the rest of the year with them by my side.

**How were you selected to speak in front of the United Nations?**

The opportunity to speak at the Youth United Nations General assembly through the teen advisor program. I have been very vocal about my support of helping missing and murdered indigenous women, and Girl Up believed that it would be a good topic to discuss at a global level. I am so glad that I have the platform to be able to speak about this issue to such a large audience and I hope to raise awareness for the cause.

**What did you present?**

The topic that I discussed was around the epidemic of missing and murdered women within the native community. Native women are murdered at a rate of 10 times the national average. As a native woman myself, I have grown to be acutely aware of this heartbreaking issue affecting Native people across the country. I discussed some statistics about missing and murdered indigenous women, presented on Savanna's act, a new bill that just recently passed the US house of representatives seeking to support reservations in their investigations of these cases, and shared some ideas on what we can all be doing to counteract this huge issue.

**Why has this issue with indigenous women not have been addressed in the past?**

It is unfortunate that the issue of missing and murdered indigenous women has not been raised to national attention. As many of the cases take place on isolated Indian reservations, many Americans are left on aware of just how prevalent the issue is. As a Native American girl Up teen advisor, I am committed to using my platform to support the native community. The intersectional oppression against women of color needs to be addressed and I hope that my speech has helped to better educate the public on what we, as a country, can be doing better.

**What is your ideal solution to this problem?**

I believe that the passing of Savanna's Act was a huge step in the right direction. We need to help support the investigations that are happening on impoverished reservations where resources are limited. The first step is helping to ensure that all these women get the justice that they deserve.

**What advice can you provide to people that feel there is an issue that needs addressing?**

I encourage you all to use your voices! You are so powerful, and you can do anything that you set your mind to. If you have personal experience with the issue, I recommend sharing your story and how it has impacted you. You got this, girl!

# TEN QUESTIONS
# WITH COVID-19
# PHYSICIAN, JULIO D.
# TORRES M.D., F.A.C.S.

J ulio D. Torres M.D., F.A.C.S. is an Otorhinolaryngolo-
gist and Head and Neck Surgeon with a practice
based in Miami-Dade Metro Area in Florida who is on
the frontlines during this COVID-19 pandemic. Dr. Julio
Torres' practice remained open during a portion of the
pandemic stay-at-home policy that was in place in light
of Florida Governor Ron DeSantis Executive Order 20-91
since the State of Florida recognized healthcare practices
as essential businesses consistent with the U.S. Dept. of

Homeland Security Guidance on the Essential Critical In-
frastructure Workforce, he closed for a period of time to
protect himself, his co-workers and his patients and pre-
pare to operate under the "new normal" of COVID-19. Dr.
Julio Torres has worked in several South Florida hospitals
and has contact with other health providers including
nurses and physicians throughout the medical field.

**How do you feel the medical field is handling COVID-19
pandemic?**

Dr. Torres' perception is that the "medical field is
doing a terrific job throughout the United States in treat-
ing and combating the COVID-19 virus," despite reports
that the United States is among the countries leading with
the most cases and deaths due to COVID-19 in the world.
Dr. Torres explains, that despite the U.S. having many
COVID-19 cases the U.S. "has per hundred thousand people
in the United States, has one of the lowest ratios in the
world." Dr. Julio Torres discussed that he had expected
there to be a larger amount of deaths in Miami than the ac-
tual number of cases. Further, he explained that the medical field expected there to be more deaths in the United
States than the present numbers demonstrating the success of the medical field's approach to this pandemic.

**As a doctor, in your opinion have you experienced hos-**

**pitals or medical practices struggling to provide care yet needing resources?**

Dr. Torres discusses, "that is a very serious problem. Personal Protection Equipment or PPE is in high demand and we could use more." Dr. Julio Torres shares the reason for the lack of PPE. He explains that the reason for the low availability of PPE is because China is one of the main manufacturers of PPE. Once the outbreak of COVID-19 began China began to limit the amount of PPE distributed to the rest of the world which began to create a shortage. Dr. Julio Torres discussed that the PPE shortage really impacted the medical field especially medical providers such as nurses and physicians that had to treat patients without the optimal protection necessary under these circumstances and without the knowledge that the patients might have contracted the COVID-19 virus which resulted in an increased number of deaths among medical workers in the field.

**What are some difficulties you have encountered with continuing to practice during the COVID-19 pandemic?**

Dr. Torres states the most glaring difficulty is the lack of Personal Protection Equipment. As a doctor focusing on the care of patients with ear, nose and throat issues, he consistently sees, "patients with symptoms such as runny nose, sore throat, and cough. It is unknown to [him] when they arrive whether the patient is suffering a cold, sinus infection, strep throat, tonsillitis which are common reasons for visits to [his] office or whether the patient has COVID-19. [They] are taking patients temperatures, but a patient might present to [his] office without a fever thereby [he] cannot focus on a high temperature reading alone to determine if it is COVID-19. [They] do not have a rapid test such as for strep throat or flu. COVID-19 is highly contagious Personal Protection Equipment is essential in order for [him] to see patients." Dr. Torres explains that it is likely that he as well as the vast majority of physicians and healthcare workers across the country have been incidentally exposed despite high levels of precautionary measures since COVID-19 testing was not readily available until late March or early April and is still not as available as necessary to protect the healthcare workers.

**What are the signs and symptoms of those ill with COVID-19?**

Dr. Julio Torres discusses that for all that have had COVID-19, it is terrifying because of the chance of having difficulty breathing or developing pneumonia or dying. Those that are candidates for testing for COVID-19 need to wait up to 7 to 8 days to receive test results. For anyone that thinks they might have COVID-19, waiting for results with no treatment could lead to the illness progressing to the point of being fatal. Dr. Julio Torres discusses that "80% of people recuperate, 20% might develop major complications, and anywhere from 12% to 13% can actually die." Some people are candidates for early treatment but others that are asymptomatic might not receive treatment while waiting for a test result. A sign that some COVID-19. Dr. Julio Torres shared that some people lose sense of smell which is an early symptom of COVID-19. Dr. Julio Torres explains that the reason COVID-19 is so terrifying is that one does not know if you are the lucky 80% that will recover or the 20% that needs to be hospitalized and may potentially die. Other signs of COVID-19 include constantly being extremely tired, no appetite, and not being able to taste food.

**What were some struggles for those medical professionals being affected with COVID-19 and later returning back to the medical practice or the frontlines in hospitals?**

Dr. Torres closed his medical practice after the stay-at-home order closures recommendations were issued for elective medical care because he found that the PPE he sought to purchase and use to be most protective for his staff and patients was completely unavailable. He did not want either his staff or himself examining patients that might have COVID-19 without proper protection. He closed his office for two weeks. Dr. Torres recounts that he felt like he needed to treat patients despite the risk of contracting COVID-19 because it this was "his war" that he was thought to fight in medical school and in his career, there had not been any pandemic to this degree. However, closing the office was quintessential because he felt like he was, "going to war without any bullets."

**What were some difficulties that came with having family members living in your house while you were still seeing patients and at risk for contracting COVID-19?**

Dr. Torres recounted that everyone in his home, including this wife, maintained social distancing including sleeping in different rooms, utilizing different bathrooms, and eating in separate areas. For maximum protection, he chooses to eat meals outside on the porch of his house and use different silverware and plates than his other family members. He maintained a distance of 6 feet or more from all family members at all times. Anyone in his home uses masks and gloves at all times in his house. Many of his colleagues in the healthcare field are doing the same. Luckily no family members in his household contracted COVID-19. However, he has not been able to see his mother since early March that is a resident at an assisted living facility due to the strict protective measures to protect assisted living facility residents from contracting COVID-19. He also has not been able to see his out of state family members.

**What is your opinion on government involvement during COVID-19?**

Dr. Julio Torres views the "United States as a victim of the lack of transparency of other countries specifically China." He continues, "in the scientific world when you make a discovery of a disease or a cure of a disease you are supposed to ethically disseminate the truth and warn everybody so the other countries and mankind will benefit." Dr. Julio Torres opines that China's lack of transparency does not only affect the United States but has also hurt the entire world.

**How did COVID-19 impact your practice?**

Once the government issued the stay-at-home orders and the number of testing increased reveling the numbers of those impacted by the pandemic, the number of patients begins to decline. This resulted in many medical practices having to temporarily furlough employees while practices were closed. However, generally, the United States given the situation, is done very well and much better than many countries in the world.

**What is your perspective on the issue of occupancy in hospitals?**

Dr. Torres shared that the medical industry knew there would be more issues with greater population densities such as New York City when combating any communicable disease equipment that can be necessary in critical cases of COVID-19 include ventilators. Dr. Torres discusses that in his home state of Florida they have adequate number of hospital beds to meet demand and they have an adequate number of ventilators, but testing is slow which remains an issue.

**The government is aiming to begin lifting stay at home orders do you believe this is the best for the United States?**

Dr. Julio Torres explains that the need for the stay-at-home order was to socially distance people especially in dense communities, make testing available, and allow time to develop treatments or vaccines. However, he believes that beginning the lifting of the stay-at-home orders is "reasonable and makes sense to open certain areas depending on the incidence of the disease." Dr. Julio Torres compared the incidence of the COVID-19 cases in Italy and the age of the population as compared to the United States. Despite Italy is a smaller country, the number of cases was high, and the average age of the population was older thereby impacting how orders would be handled. In the U.S., there are states that have had very few cases of COVID-19 and in many residents' point of view, the economic impact of staying at home and not working outweighs the risk of contracting COVID-19 where there are so few cases. Dr. Torres states even in areas with a low number of cases, or areas that lift the stay-at-home orders, people still need to follow precautionary measures such as safer-at-home, continue social distancing, washing hands, and taking other the necessary precautions but he states, "it makes perfect sense to open certain areas to get the economy moving again depending on the prevalence of the COVID-19 cases." Healthcare works will continue to be in the frontlines, providing care for those impacted by COVID-19.

# TEN QUESTIONS WITH CWCC BUSINESS DEVELOPMENT MANAGER, MORGAN MONTGOMERY

**M**organ Montgomery is originally from Colorado and attended West Virginia University, receiving her Sport Management and Business Administration degrees. Her passions lie in women in sports and empowerment, which eventually led her to the Colorado Women's Chamber of Commerce (CWCC), working there for two and a half years. Only 24, she is the current Business Development Manager and Sales and Marketing Coordinator. She meets with influential business owners or members of corporations. In the Denver, Colorado area, she helps empower women and grow their careers. Although her interests lie in sports management, Montgomery has found it exciting to transition out of a male dominated industry into a profession focused on supporting and empowering women while building the economy in Colorado.

**What is your career and day to day?**

I am the business development manager for the Colorado Women's Chamber of Commerce, which essentially means I run all of our memberships and partnerships. We are an organization where small business owners, as well as women, corporations, or large companies, can get involved. We have about 425 members with about 2000 representatives that we serve out of those. My day-to-day pre-COVID, I would say I worked from a coffee shop where I was constantly meeting members, or I was at their offices, connecting with them, finding ways for them to get involved. Whether they were a member of the chamber and wanted to get involved in our programming or just learning about it and wanting to know what our community was about. Now, nine months later, I am mostly on zoom meetings still with those members, I attend zoom events, I am all about getting the mission of the women's chamber out there and helping our current members still engage because we moved in March fully from an in-person community to an entirely virtual community. I focus on helping our members always know that they can engage within the chamber, even if they're not necessarily in-person going to events.

**What is your philosophy in your work?**

I think for me, it's what you can give. How can you keep getting people involved? How can you lift one another up? We had a member a year or so ago who created a really cool graphic, which was of a woman. She was lifting one hand up to the woman in front of her and putting one hand down to the woman beneath her, creating this chain of how we all are lifting each other because we value that there is no kind of my way your way. This collective of how we can all ride and all make Colorado in Denver the place for women in business. How can we recreate that on a national level? I would say it's about what can you give? How can I be there for the members we serve and for the women we serve and make sure that they feel empowered the most.

**How has COVID-19 effected your work?**

Directly COVID-19 has affected my work because I

can no longer attend events; I was at events probably two or three times a week. I work from home now, which is kind of nice. My job has changed to that I'm still meeting with people, but now virtually, but still making connections. Instead of focusing on bringing new members into the Chamber, we're focused right now on the members we have; of course, adding people to the Chamber is important. We're focused on hunkering down and helping the members we do have, whether with PPP, small business loans, even just supporting them as they navigate now working from home. Whether that's with kids at home, adjusting to not going to the office and isolation.

**The Colorado Woman's Chamber of Commerce, empowers women especially in business, but what is its mission?**

Our mission is to advance women in business, whether they're business owners, in a company, or a corporation. The vision is to put Colorado on the map as the place for women in business. What we do is the empowerment education of women through different programs. We have leadership programs and mentorship programs; we've got luncheons that we do, which, of course, are virtual right now. Small groups focus on whether you're an entrepreneur or a woman in a corporation and content-based groups: business development, growth, health, and wellness. We do wealth and investment, so full-range services there as well. We are the Women's Chamber of

Commerce, but it's about 85% female, 15% male, so really focus on also finding male champions in the workplace, who can be there as mentors or allies for women in business, because we realize that it is not us versus them. It is a collective of how we're all working together, but going to be more focused on our chamber, specifically on the growth of women in their careers in their businesses.

## How were you able to overcome these struggles?

I think the biggest way that we were able to overcome some of the struggles was leaning on the team. I am on a team of three, and then a couple of contractors focus on reaching out to them. I also think it was relying on our members; we have awesome members involved in the women's chamber. It was really cool to see how they were pivoting and getting energy from how they were making the transition and being able to say, 'hey, how can we help?' I think the biggest way I overcame it was admitting when it was hard for myself, making sure that I was there supporting other women, and just taking a deep breath. I think the hardest part was when you work from home and your commute goes from your bed to your couch or your bed to your desk; you can work from 6 am to 8 pm. So really creating those boundaries of at five o'clock, I'm done working or six o'clock, whatever it may be. If I have to run late, then the next morning, I might sleep in and take care of my mental health. I needed to make sure I was still serving the community that we work in really well.

## How has your marketing strategy been changed or influenced by the COVID-19 pandemic?

I'd say the probably the biggest way we've changed our marketing is, as I mentioned, where we're with the women's Chamber of Commerce had always been a 100% in person, kind of a group. It was how you have to show up to benefit from it, or that was the philosophy. One weekend in March, when the pandemic really hit and everything shut down, we realized if we didn't become a virtual community where people could connect, we probably weren't going to make it very far through the chamber or the pandemic. We knew we had too many people who relied on our services or the community we created. So, our marketing became, 'how do you plug in virtually? What does a zoom meeting look like? How do you keep a zoom meeting?' I think the shift in our marketing really was it became member focus, and not that it never was before, but before it was, here's this event and here's this that we're doing.

We launched two kinds of new initiatives; one was women crushing Wednesday, which, of course, is about highlighting our women in our community and what they're doing. It really was member focus, and how are we highlighting, especially, businesses that were struggling due to the pandemic, or how were they pivoting? Then we also started Girls Club, which became our Monday motivation of how we are kicking off listening to one of our members or a powerful female in the community. How they're making that transition? Our marketing became about elevating other women and making sure that they're lifted up, sharing their story, and providing that inspiration. Our large-scale events where we have 500 to 800 people could no longer happen unless in a virtual setting. We focused on elevating an individual or a company and how they were taking advantage of it.

We had quite a few companies that had no idea what they were going to do, whether they were like us, and we're mostly in person. We had quite a few restaurant owners and other things like that, so it became about how we are all pivoting. It shifted to showing off how women are flexible and can transition in the face of a global pandemic, rise and grow their businesses, and elevate their careers. We had many women who took promotions or were able to grow their careers and companies that they were in, even if they were shifting to that kind of work from home model.

**How's the chamber been helping women during this pandemic, especially when there's been so much job loss?**

"When the layoffs hit initially, we had quite a few hotels that were involved, which, of course, their business went to nearly zero overnight. The airport is a member of ours and became focused on PPP loans. We made sure that we partnered with the SBA, Small Business Association, to ensure they were getting the resources they needed, whether applying for the PPP loans or anything else. Exclusively, we have a foundation that we work with that's launching in 2021, which will be able to do more fundraising and help on the monetary side.

In terms of job loss, it was making sure that they still felt like they had a community. We didn't cut any memberships; we actually offered memberships to people who hadn't had one before so that they could get engaged. Whether it was staying involved in our corporate women's track or making sure they were still making connections at potentially other companies. We were really opening our arms to everybody could be involved in our programming. The first three months of the pandemic, we actually opened up so that everybody could be a part of the chamber.

The other piece that we did was focus on making sure people again go back to that community and give them the resources they need. Now we did webinars on mental health, childcare, and how you are dealing with having your kids at home. They can't go to school or daycare, but many still are potentially working for eight hours.

We try to provide that support behind everything and promoting businesses. We connected many of our small businesses that were restaurants to our larger companies like health care workers. So really, finding ways to creatively make sure that our members could still make money or grow. I think being that support system, we called about every one of our members in those first couple of weeks that the pandemic hit to hear what they needed. Quite a few of them didn't have time to talk to us because they were in the middle of a transition and needed to focus on their own companies. But it was trying to make sure that they knew we were still there, and they could come to us for whatever they needed, and we could probably find a connection.

**Earlier, you said that the Chamber was focusing on its members, but at the same time, you allowed everyone to join the Chamber. So, did you see a dramatic increase in your members, or did it stay pretty consistent?**

I would say in terms of the members that we have right now. We saw engagement rise a lot. It was because they didn't have to commute to one of our groups or were looking for community. I think it was simply you're sitting in your house many times, whether it's with your immediate family or alone. They were looking for a community, and it was an easier process because all they had to do was log on to zoom.

In terms of new members, we had quite a few that joined each month. I think almost every company we had income, or revenue loss, which we knew was coming. We were prepared for quite a few of our larger companies that joined and wanted to get heavily involved, whether on our board or just getting their employees involved. We saw quite a few larger companies that potentially didn't have the same kind of revenue hit or could still generate money join the Chamber. We also ironically saw quite a few small businesses who were looking for community, wanting to be involved in something, or just needing the resources we could provide; we had them join. We've never had been an organization that if you can't pay, you can't be involved. We always work with people who want to get involved. So that was something where I was a lot of what I was doing was figuring out. So the process became a lot less rigid. We made sure that it was beneficial, whether we traded. We pretty much hit all of the goals that we readjusted to and still kind of stay afloat in that world. Our biggest revenue hit was on the event side because we usually have four large signature events throughout the year, and we were only able to do one in February this year.

For the most part, membership stayed strong. The renewals were coming in, people who are current members continue to stay on with us. I would say there was growth in many different ways, whether it was engagement or members.

**Can you provide an example of a specific situation that COVID impacted a project and how you were able found a solution to overcome it?**

I think the most significant way that COVID impacted us was through large scale events. We've got one, the one that we were able to have in February is an 800-person event, which we barely squeaked in there before the world's shut down. Then we have three others. For those, it became whether or not people would sit for a two-hour event on their computers and how do we interact, create ways for it still to be interesting, and be relevant. We wanted to provide people the opportunity to connect with other people. We incorporated breakout rooms brought in powerful speakers to keep us connected. We did intros, so even if there were 100 people on the zoom call, you could still connect with three or four of them. You could use the chat function to get your questions answered. When we were in-person, you would raise your hand, and we would go around the room. One of our events, Girls Rising, focuses on getting young women into non-traditional careers. We provide scholarships with our community partners that we work with, we honor the women that get the scholarships, and we bring in speakers to talk in those different kinds of non-traditional for us. We focused on engineering, technology, entrepreneurship, trade skills, and construction this year. We focused on women going into those careers and how we can support them. Girls Rising was our first signature event that we created this virtual world for, and it worked out well. We still had enough individuals to honor the women who were getting the scholarships and still feel like a community. I think it's always a learning experience with COVID of understanding the event worked well virtually than doing our health and wellness group outside.

We were constantly pivoting, but I hate to overuse the word. We started using the phrase swivel because we were not pivoting and changing what we were doing. We just swiveled to continue what we were doing more safely for our members. Towards the end of the year, we were hoping to have some of our smaller groups meet in person again, which then the second wave of COVID hit. But it became, how are you rolling with this COVID situation. Everything that happened with the social climate this year involved pivoting, our events to speak to women, women of color, men of color, LGBTQ, everything that was going on this year, and then adding the political theme. This year was about swiveling and figuring out how relevant you are when something like a global pandemic hits. You have to figure out if our members still want to engage. Does our community still value us? Do people still want to engage? I think that's the beautiful part of this year. We found out that the women's Chamber is significant to people in the community, and people rely on us for quite a few different things. It hurt that we had to change everything we were doing, which was scary for a long time. It showed the community that we're building here is pretty strong because everyone stepped up in the face of something that the majority of us have never seen. Hopefully, we'll never see again in a global pandemic.

**How has the Colorado Woman's Chamber of Commerce specifically been impacted by the pandemic?**

COVID specifically impacted the Chamber because we could no longer have our large-scale events, which hits us economically. Still, also it hurts when you can't have those events when you're getting together with people, and you get to see people. As someone who goes to events all the time, I was craving connection with members of our community, but they're also open to the public. We had to be creative in figuring out how to market what the women's Chamber is doing without necessarily having those public events where people could come in and see what we're doing firsthand. That was a specific way that COVID directly impacted the women's Chamber like many others we've said. Previously, the shutdowns impacted our revenue, but members started to get deeply involved in our community.

Instead of being fully in-person community, if you had a meeting or couldn't make one of our meetings, you could plugin. We had events throughout the day at different times to see what works best for people. People could take a break from what they were doing with their jobs to come to a woman chamber event virtually, which was fantastic to see our community rally around. Whereas usually in our events, we're all dressed up nicely. We got to see inside people's homes, had kids joining, and had dogs popping up into meetings. It's cool how our community became stronger because we got to see each other as our authentic selves. We got to how women genuinely operate. Women are often the number one caregiver at home, so that became my kids playing Legos in the corner, one of my favorite meetings I had the little kid just came over and was like, Mom, I need you. She fixed it, and he went about his business. I think that's really where the women's Chamber has switched to having a lot more grace for what we're doing. Women can show up as their authentic selves, and we're doing it all virtually.

Our impact has grown where we had a couple of women from Wyoming and outside the Denver Metro area get involved in what we were doing. Whereas now, we'll always have a virtual component to what we're doing so that people outside of Denver and Colorado can still engage. It was hard at first. We knew we would take a revenue hit, and for a small business, revenue hits are hard to navigate because we're already running on kind of lower resources. But it was a way to see the importance of the Chamber.

# TEN QUESTIONS WITH POLSINELLI SHAREHOLDER AND AWARD WINNING LITIGATOR, GHISLAINE G. TORRES BRUNER

**G**hislaine G. Torres Bruner, Esq. grew up in South Florida and attended Ransom Everglades School in Coconut Grove for high school. She always knew that she wanted to have a career that involved public health. Bruner volunteered to assist children with various disabilities at a young age and worked at Mercy Hospital during her junior and senior high school years.

Upon graduating from high school, Bruner attended The University of Michigan in Ann Arbor and obtained an interdisciplinary Bachelor of Science degree in Women's Health. She focused her studies on women's biological, psychological, and social makeup to better improve women's opportunities. Her coursework included developmental biology, endocrinology, physics, biochemistry, sociology, neuropsychology, anthropology, women's studies, and Latin American studies. Bruner became fascinated by issues involving environmental and social impacts upon women, so she decided to pursue a Master of Science in Public Health with a concentration in environmental health and safety.

During her Master of Public Health coursework, she studied epidemiology, statistics, industrial hygiene, and environmental health. This course study gave her a strong basis in understanding environmental factors such as air quality and water quality, which led her to pursue in-depth studies on how environmental and occupational hazards and pollution could impact maternal and child health. During her public health studies, Bruner had an opportunity to work at a medical practice. She became interested in health policy and issues such as fraud, abuse, and reimbursements. She became interested in health policy and laws surrounding health care.

After much discussion with several professors, Bruner decided that the career that overlapped laws and policy, health, and the environment, was law. She attended law school in South Florida and began practicing law there. Bruner represented physicians, nurses, hospitals, and nursing homes in medical-legal actions and practiced there for about 5-6 years and then had the opportunity to move to Denver.

When Bruner arrived in Colorado, she quickly learned that it was the energy industry's epicenter— with a growing oil and gas industry. Bruner wanted to know more about the energy sector and oil and gas development, so after practicing law for about nine years, she decided to obtain a master's in law degree in Environmental Health and Policy from the University of Denver, Sturm College of Law. She realized that her strong science and public health foundation had paved the way for a legal practice in natural resources law and energy litigation, which is her current focus.

Bruner is currently a shareholder in Polsinelli P.C.'s commercial litigation and energy practice. Bruner is licensed and works in Colorado, Florida, New Mexico, North

Dakota, Utah, and Wyoming in Energy litigation. Bruner has represented individuals at the state, national, and international levels due to her broad range of experience. Bruner was featured as Colorado Law Weekly's "2020 Top Litigator", and as a 2020's Barister's Best. Bruner's law experience pertains to Commercial Litigation; Energy, Environmental, and Real Estate Litigation; Energy Regulatory, and Transactional Practice.

Bruner is the Vice-Chair of the American Bar Association for Articles for Energy, Environmental, and Resources for the Oil and Gas Committee. Bruner is a Member of the Women's Energy Network and serves on the Colorado Oil and Gas Association's Local Regulatory Committee; EHSR Committee; and Legal, Legislative, and Regulatory Committee. Bruner was named a "Top Woman in Energy" and "Who's Who in Energy" in 2018 and 2019 by the Denver Business Journal.

**What is your career, and what do you do for your work?**

I am an energy litigation and natural resources lawyer. I represent various oil and gas and other energy companies in their planning or permitting of contentious projects or projects that occur in sensitive areas, whether there in urban or suburban communities or near environmentally sensitive areas. I assist my clients in obtaining a social license to operate within the communities they plan to operate. Communities have different expectations and needs, and I help energy companies navigate those regulatory processes while understanding the communities needs and expectations. I look at environmental impacts and whether there are mitigations that can help protect public health or reduce inconveniences of nuisances due to the temporary construction of these projects. I have to work with engineers, environmental and regulatory professionals that know the technical side of their projects and place the laws, regulations and community expectations side-by-side. I also assist physicians in the health care field and other individuals in shareholder disputes and litigation.

**What is your philosophy in your work?**

My philosophy on work is that you need to be available for your clients anytime when their needs may arise. You need to be a trusted advisor and treat all clients with great respect and consideration. Every client is important and a gift. Cultivating and preserving your relationship with them is as essential as a great work product.

**How has COVID-19 affected your work?**

I was used to regularly meeting with my clients in person and learning about their projects. I was also used to attending hearings, depositions, and trials in person in whatever state the court I was before was located. This was a valuable part of practicing law because there is so much that can be interpreted by the courtroom's dynamic. Since the start of COVID-19, we have not been able to have in-person meetings with our clients. Furthermore, we have had to hold most of our court hearings virtually or telephonically and depositions, which have been challenging. While most trials have been postponed or delayed, I did have an in-person trial in October of 2020 in which we had to socially distance and wear masks for extended periods. We had to find new ways to introduce evidence without approaching witnesses.

We have had to become experts in holding virtual meetings efficiently, presenting evidence for depositions via various virtual platforms. We have had to deal with the challenges of talking over ourselves and handling a workday in 8-10 hours; it now takes about 14-16 hours due to connectivity issues, handling many tasks supported by in-office expert personnel on our own.

Also, many companies we represent had to file for Chapter 11 bankruptcy to reorganize, reduce debt or sell assets. Other companies had to cut back expenses and thereby not requiring as much legal work as they had in the past.

## How were you able to overcome these struggles?

The way I have overcome these struggles is to become technologically savvy or at least proficient. Holding telephonic depositions or hearings was not wholly unheard of turn the last 19 years of my practice; it usually occurred on occasion and was not preferred or the norm. Now, it has become standard practice. When we hold the court hearings on the phone, it is sometimes difficult not to talk over each other. When attending the hearings virtually, we have to try not to talk over each other it sometimes becomes awkward to get the statements in. However, it also depends on how the judge runs his courtroom. On one occasion, I felt like the motion calendar in one of my South Florida cases ran smoother than ever before.

When the stay-at-home orders went into place, COVID-19 pushed off most of my trials indefinitely. One of my trials took place in October 2020. It was incredibly nerve-wrecking to think that we would expose our team, clients as well as witnesses to COVID-19. Fortunately, we had no cases arise. But the stress was nonetheless real. We had to use masks, and it was difficult to breathe when we were arguing motions or conducting cross-examinations. On one occasion, one of my co-counsel nearly passed out from the lack of oxygen with the mask. However, the good news is through lots of preparation and practice; we overcame challenges by devoting time to preparing for virtual depositions and socially distanced trials.

## How has your marketing strategy been changed or influenced by the COVID-19 pandemic?

The pandemic has impacted our legal practices because it is driven by client development and referrals. By not being in social gatherings, it is sometimes difficult to secure new work. However, it has led us to develop in the various areas to contact clients through virtual happy hours, webinars, podcasts, blogs, the use of social media, writing, and other engagement.

## Can you provide an example of a specific situation in that COVID impacted a project and how you found a solution to overcome it?

A specific challenge was how we were going to run the trial period; we decided to rearrange the courtroom to be socially distanced. Instead of using a podium, we remained at our desks or memorized the material so we could speak without notes being placed in any particular place. We also used music stands as podiums so that we could have our space. We also made binders for the witnesses and left them on the witness stand with the various documents we might have to cross-examine, impeach them, or conduct our examination. It proved actually to be quite efficient. We also discussed the cases with opposing counsel and established several facts to stipulate to run a more efficient trial and have fewer witnesses. I think in the end, we cut about two days of trial time instead of adding which previously was a concern.

**How has COVID specifically impacted your law firm during the pandemic?**

My law firm has over 20 offices across the country. We often traveled from office to office to get to know our fellow partners and work on cases or attend conferences. This was important because it strengthened the firm culture. We also used to have many gatherings in our offices set up in a more modern open plan. Following the stay-at-home orders, we had to stop traveling, and we were no longer able to use our office for gatherings. This wasn't easy because clients and organizations counted on us to have these types of events.

However, from a day-to-day in-person operation, we transitioned online seamlessly. Since we could always move around to other offices, our attorneys were equipped to work remotely. However, some of our support staff had to be transitioned. I recall distinctly that we closed on March 12th at around 3:00 PM, and by March 13th at 9:00 AM, I was up and running from home as if nothing happened. Our intra-firm meetings have increased, and I think it has strengthened our firm culture across all offices and practice groups. I anticipate that in the coming years, states will realize that we have the ability to reside in one state and appear in court in another easily.

**How have you been able to cope with separation from others for an extended period; do you have any advice for those who might be struggling?**

I arrange weekly calls with many of the team members that help me with my cases. We discuss what is coming up with the cases and any necessary work period; this is great because we can see each other face to face when we set them up via Zoom, WebEx, or other similar means. We also prepared unique gifts for the Holidays. The advice that I have for those who might be struggling is to find some way to interact with others. I went back to playing tennis, which, while I'm alone on my side of the court, I at least engage in an activity with somebody on the other side. Likewise, I have held various virtual events for my firm, and I've partnered with other non-profit organizations I work with to promote engagement.

**What advice do you have for teenagers preparing for their future careers?**

I would advise teens two make an effort to learn how to move through transitions smoothly. Life has a lot of changes and shifts, and it is necessary to be flexible. I would also tell teens that they need to make an effort to set up organizational systems in place that account for any changes in circumstances.

**What advice would you give to teenagers that are having difficulties discovering what career they would live to pursue? What advice would you give to someone aspiring for your career?**

I would tell teenagers who are having difficulty discovering or career to pursue to try to do various volunteer jobs whether they be member tool or social distance opportunities. It is essential to identify what skills you are good at, whether you are good at writing, speaking, planning, or creating things. Not everybody is the same, and it is vital to identify what skills you like and be willing to do repeatedly.

For someone aspiring to be a lawyer, I would advise them to be willing to work under pressure and be organized. You should also be ready to work as a team. I would also recommend that they take classes in communications or public speaking to learn to manage and deliver a message. I would also recommend the pursuit of economics courses to understand the markets. A lot of what I do in energy, specifically in oil and gas, is somewhat contingent on the commodity markets and supply and demand. I would encourage an aspiring attorney to follow trends in innovation. Likewise, I would advise that they need to learn how to write contracts and draft briefs. The two go hand in hand. An attorney who has drafted an agreement is somewhat situated better to defend the deal because they may understand the terms more closely. I would also obtain some underlining expertise to have a dedicated and specific practice area. It was helpful that I was knowledgeable in public health and chemistry, and when coming to Denver, it led me to energy law. Last, I would tell the individual that law can be a lot of fun if you create a balance.

# TEN QUESTIONS WITH GROWTH AND PERFORMANCE MARKETING EXPERT, GINELLE TORRES

G inelle Torres, originally from Miami, Florida, studied print journalism and English at Florida International University. Later, she worked as a reporter at the Miami Herald and South Florida Sun-Sentinel. After many years, Torres moved to Los Angeles, pursuing marketing and advertising. She has worked in numerous industries in consumer product goods and entertainment throughout her career, with Ticketmaster, Nutri Ninja, and Murad.

Torres is a strong Digital Marketing strategist driving to date nearly $3 billion gross revenue for the companies she has worked with throughout her career. She is well-versed in the social media realm, especially with advertising on Instagram and YouTube.

**What is your career and what do you do for your work?**

I'm currently the Director of Growth & Performance Marketing for a clean beauty company, where I drive our strategy and execution across digital marketing.

**What is your philosophy in your work?**

Stay focused, work hard and always be thinking long term.

**How has COVID-19 affected your work?**

We have been working remotely since March, which has impacted the interpersonal relationships across the company, communication, and building strong team dynamics or team building. Zoom fatigue has hit us hard, as it takes away being able to meet in person, grab coffee and even brainstorm. Many of us have worked hard to build relationships as best we can.

**How were you able to overcome these struggles?**

It is a constant challenge. Trying to set up one-on-one time with colleagues or even a 30 min meeting where work isn't talked about to help us become better teammates and not leave us feeling so isolated.

**How has your marketing strategy been changed or influenced by the COVID-19 pandemic?**

We have had to pivot to keep in mind issues hitting mankind. Furloughs, unemployments, depressions, suicides, etc. It's important to be aware of the difficulties and challenges hitting our world.

**How have you been able to cope with separation from others for an extended period of time and do you have any advice for those who might be struggling?**

Talk to your close friends and family. Human connection is important. If you feel you're struggling a lot, then reach out to a mental health specialist. there are great apps to help you relax and unwind such as Headspace which helps you stay calm. In addition, cardio workouts, yoga, stay in motion, it helps clear the mind and endorphins are especially important during this time. Going on walks with your friends and family (masks on of course) is great as well. Being able to chat on long walks helps you stay mentally strong.

**How has marketing been changed or altered as a result of the pandemic?**

The pandemic has brought both opportunities and challenges for marketers. On the positive side, it's allowed us to be more creative with how we communicate messages to consumers taking into account the state of the world. We rely on more emotive angels vs. straight-forward approaches. Some of the challenges are articulating and positioning brands and products, while many are not working or are suffering. There has to be a good balance of being empathetic while driving our goals.

Another positive is how consumers are ingesting media. We have the opportunity to reach them at a higher frequency on OTT (over-the-top marketing such as streaming, cable, applications, and more), digital audio, including podcasts and Spotify. This allows us to tell more thoughtful stories and capture our audience where they're the most active.

**Given the changes due to the pandemic, what advice do**

**you have for individuals in the marketing profession currently struggling with adapting to culture changes from COVID-19?**

I encourage marketers to take a personal approach towards developing marketing strategies during this time. What would pull at your heartstrings? What would offend you? What would encourage you to make a purchase? If you feel it would work for you, then chances are, it would work for others, too! Also, use this time to continue your education. Take online courses and brush up on your analytics and data insights, story-telling, presentation skills. This is a great time to leverage your remote work schedule and lack of a commute (if you're so fortunate) to take that time to nourish your mind and even explore other facets of marketing you've wanted to know more about.

**What advice do you have for teenagers preparing for their future careers?**

This is a challenging time to be making decisions for your future and career but it's a great time to be setting goals and have options. My best piece of advice is have a plan and a backup plan! The world is changing everyday and having a few options will keep you working towards something with alternatives should anything have to change. Be comfortable knowing that your main goal might shift, and that's ok. Also, learn to study and work remotely, it may be how things continue for several years. Setting up a proper work space or study space, where you can focus, with minimal distractions is key to successfully live in the new remote world. Be good at maintaining a schedule and taking breaks. Digital detoxes on the weekends will work wonders! Put down the devices and spend time outdoors.

**What advice would you give to teenagers that are having difficulties discovering what career they would live to pursue? What advice would you give to someone aspiring for your career?**

This is a good time to figure out a few career options, perhaps in a couple of industries. Think if you will be able to thrive in a remote work situation or if you need to be in an office environment. Where and how can you intern? If you attend grad school, where can you work to help get work experience? Backup plans are key right now. Having a couple of alternatives will not only make things more flexible for you but also a desirable candidate when it comes time to apply for various positions.

For someone with an interest in Digital Marketing - take math classes and learn all you can in analytics. There's a lot of data and finance that goes into my role, and it's important to know how to manage a budget and also be able to analyze the impact that your work has on the company! Brand studies are also great to have and understand. Interning is very important. In order to get a job right out of college, you'll need to have real world experience. Start applying as soon as your first semester is coming to a close when you have an idea of industries that have gotten your interest. Also, it's great to intern across the board, it will help you know what you like and what you don't like. Focus on working on areas where you're passionate, that will keep you excited to work everyday!

# TEN QUESTIONS WITH I AM REMARKABLE GOLD TIER TRAINER AND GCC BUSINESS COACH STEPHANIE SHIVER-HOGAN

S tephanie Shiver-Hogan, located in Denver, Colorado, initially pursued a Bachelor's Degree in International Business and Finance at the University of Colorado, Denver. Since then, she has done further studies towards obtaining a Master's Degree from the University of Denver. Later on, she was certified by the International Coaching Federation in Business coaching. For the last two decades, Shiver-Hogan has worked in finance, accounting, related healthcare, insurance, marketing, and many more. She is currently pursuing a PCC—higher level of Coaching administered by the International Coaching Federation (ICF). Shiver-Hogan works with leaders in industries, especially Chief Executive Officers on Fortune 500s, entrepreneurs, and large organizations: Merrill Lynch, AIG (Formerly Chartis), Northwestern Mutual, and Pulte Homes. Later she founded Gallantry Coaching and Consulting to aid individuals in the business realm, emphasizing stability in her approach to business practices.

**What is your career?**

I am an executive coach and a consultant with Gallantry Coaching and Consulting. I work with executives, and business owners, to help them to tackle business challenges or opportunities that they have within their practice. But more specifically, I'm a 12 Week Year certified trainer, a book that Brian Moran and Michael Lennington wrote. I help my clients use those methodologies to become more efficient and effective, professionally and personally. They can find more space to either go after big, hairy audacious goals or to find more balance, maybe between their personal and professional lives.

**What is your day to day?**

Generally, I'd meet with clients, most days of the week before the pandemic, either over the phone or over zoom. So that had minimal impact. We also do small group coaching, which is best facilitated over zoom. So that hasn't changed much. I am a professional speaker as well. When the pandemic hit, we rescheduled several speaking engagements. We've transitioned to an online platform. I'm learning how to do a lot more training and teaching speaking over zoom and other virtual media.

**What is your philosophy in your work?**

My philosophy is to help individuals reach their greatest potential to uncover areas that will help them become a better version of themselves.

**How has COVID-19 most impacted your work?**

The speaking engagements in person have changed. In my professional work, I have a personal mission to introduce ten people in my network to one another for their benefit. I'm not looking to get anything out of it; if I can introduce good people to other good people, great things happen. In the past, I was networking and meeting with people regularly in person, but that has become more challenging. It's taken on a new angle. Now, I'm out there kind of shaking hands with individuals remotely and figuring out how I can continue to network in a virtual world, which is very different than in person. But I think it's vital work. We have had to pivot; that's become the word of the year regarding how we have tackled issues. It is such an essential part of my personal and professional passion.

**How are you able to overcome struggles caused by the COVID pandemic?**

I think pivoting has been critical and being okay with change. Another excellent book recommendation is Who Moved My Cheese; it's a great book and very relevant for where we stand today. How do I become part of the formula versus being so focused on what we're doing today? I see a challenge within my relationship with some of my clients because we're so head down and trying to figure out what we're doing today that we need to step back and look at the vision of the future and be more progressive so we can anticipate. For me, it's been about being agile, being on my toes, and being open to new opportunities; I think those things have been critical to the success of where it is that my business has gone. One of the things that I do is talk in my practice a lot; not only am I a certified trainer, but I am an avid reader. I think reading is so critical and so important. I spend a lot of time understanding it but figuring out how it applies to conversations with others. I encourage people to use other tools outside of conversations with me, share some information to grow.

**Can you provide an example of a specific situation in that COVID impacted a project and how you were able to find a solution to overcome it?**

One specific thing that comes to mind, I was invited to participate in a fireside chat with an industry-specific group. I want to say it initially was scheduled sometime in May or April. Right after COVID sent us home, I got notification from them that they tried to cancel and that we were going to reconsider rescheduling. I jumped on the phone with the lady who ran that organization and said, "Hey, what's the plan? What are you thinking?" She said, "Well, we're not sure; we don't know what we're doing." There was a lot of uncertainty at that time.

We eventually peeled back the onion to figure out what was ailing her and what she had heard from some of her organization members. We quickly pivoted, and I created a new session. We went from announcement to launch within four days. I want to say we had a conversation on a Wednesday, she published it to her constituents or group members on a Thursday, and I taught the class on Monday, and over 100 people attended. It's really about giving people who had recently moved to an at-home work environment some tools that they can execute right away. I don't remember when it was exactly, but I want to say this, even maybe before the end of March, or very early April, was when people had a lot of uncertainty. I thought that was about to get great feedback. How do you have 100 people show up to a session you created and marketed within a few business days? The message was relevant and essential for that period and has turned into some business opportunities for me. I think something great came out of it both on my side and her side from just being open to the possibility of maybe not necessarily following the rules but trying to figure out how we can make an impact and quickly.

**What advice would you have for teenagers that are just beginning to network?**

Practice makes perfect. I would say getting out and practicing networking, whether that's a conversation with a teacher, professor, another student, a parent of a friend, as you get older, it gets more challenging. I can tell you many clients find it very awkward because they were never taught or didn't understand the value of networking when they were younger. Now that they're older, it's not ingrained in them to have a conversation. Becoming comfortable with asking people for their time or having a conversation with them is critical. There's a book that I would strongly recommend; it's called The Defining Decade: Why Your Twenties Matter And How to Make the Most of Them Now by Meg Jay. She also has a TED talk, which I highly recommend. But if I'm in my late teens or 20s, I think reading this book can have such a profound impact on your future. Specifically, a chapter discusses loose connections, the importance of being connected with people, and how we naturally want to help others. I think there is a particular chapter that is very powerful. It's about understanding how networking can open doors or the opportunities you can gain by having enough gumption or bravery, or enthusiasm to take the risk of meeting other people and connecting with them.

## How does your business consulting intertwine with I am remarkable?

I Am Remarkable is a Google initiative created internally in Google to help women and then later expanded to all minorities. I would say it's to enable them to use their voice for self-promotion. I am a certified as a gold tier certified trainer is the exact title with the I Am Remarkable. Still, we use it to connect with women, specifically in our network, and some other minority groups to help them find their voice. We also help them recognize some of the challenges and opportunities surrounding self-promotion of ourselves and supporting others' self-promotion.

**I Am Remarkable works with women and minorities, but what advice would you have for them and teenagers to self-promote themselves?**

I would say going back to Meg Jay's book, *The Defining Decade*. I think it's very relevant and a great reference. You also have to practice getting in front of people. Regarding self-promotion, I think getting comfortable with who you are and what you present is essential. One of the things that we talk about in my practice is your values. If you are clear on who you are, it's easy for you to communicate that to others. So, understanding your values and what's important to you, I think it's critical. I think getting comfortable with having conversations with other people from a networking perspective. The success of being able to self-promote in Meg Jay's book is called *Weak Ties*.

One of the things that we talk about in I Am Remarkable is how we support others in their self-promotion. How our skills help us promote ourselves, and how are we acting when other people are self-promoting? As we talked about, self-promotion is if you and I were to carry a conversation and self-promote ourselves in the process, which can manifest itself in words like gloating or bragging. How do we create space for others to tell their truth, which in some cases might be self-promotion? The challenge or opportunity for us is that individuals who have been in oppressed situations are less efficient, effective, or skilled in self-promotion. We not only need to teach those folks how to garner that skill and practice it. How do we support those individuals in their practice and help them create a platform to be okay with promoting themselves and not being shut down?

**What advice would you give to teenagers that are having difficulties discovering what career they would like to pursue? What advice would you give someone aspiring for your career?**

Stop worrying. For the love of peace, stop worrying about what you want to be when you grow up. Because I, even in my world, I have changed my career. Human resource professionals have a conversation with the recruiter and freak out because they can't put me in a box. That's the most significant benefit to the work that I do today because I don't just have one skill set; I don't have one thing I've done in my background. That's not to say that the people who find their passion shouldn't go after it with vigor and enthusiasm, but if you don't know today, who cares! As I mentioned at the beginning, your journey is through your education, your experiences, and the opportunities presented to you. Another great book, *The Luck Factor*, talks about how people get lucky, and there's a formula around that and understanding that. Luck is just a product of putting yourself out there and allowing yourself to be encountered with luck and more options to take advantage of or experiences you could potentially be exposed to. I would say it's super important to be okay with not exactly knowing what the future holds. There are plenty of clients that I have that are in their 30s, 40s, and 50s. That still can't answer the question, what do I want to do when I grow up? Please don't feel so much pressure as a teenager or 20 something that you have to know the answer, explore and ask questions when given the opportunity. What are you studying? What do you think that you want to learn? For example, I want to explore this because if you converse with those people, they will open up your eyes to new things that you didn't even know existed. If someone had told me in high school that I would be an executive coach as an adult, I would have laughed in their face. So, stop trying so hard to figure out the end game, and enjoy the journey.

# TEN QUESTIONS WITH REMAX REALTOR, LEAH WHITE

G rowing up, Leah White witnessed as many of her family members partook in the Real Estate profession. They took advantage of opportunities to buy houses for their descendants, which inspired White to pursue opportunities in the real estate arena. White discussed how she witnessed her grandmother's career flourish in California while Real Estate was prosperous. During that time, a surge in new construction projects throughout the state occurred. As a young girl, White assisted her grandmother by passing out flyers at the local markets.

Later on, White married, had children and left the state of California. While her children were young, she remained a stay-at-home mom, but as they grew older and became independent, she obtained her license and returned to her passion, Real Estate.

Through real estate, White has been allowed to aid people every day. She does not perceive her career as purely buying and selling houses but assisting people in moving on to the next stage of their lives. White expresses her genuine joy in helping people through her profession. White's greatest pleasure is to witness the pure happiness she brings to her clients when they close on a property and move into the new home. White also enjoys helping people purchase investment properties, similar to her grandfather.

Throughout this unprecedented year, she has continued to help people purchase properties even through these extenuating circumstances. She has maintained her motivation by continuously reflecting on her vision board she created in partnership with I Am Remarkable, which aids women in business and workplace ventures.

Numerous businesses in the Real Estate realm have collapsed due to the struggles generated by the COVID-19 pandemic. However, White has concluded this year with great triumphs due to her outstanding leadership, work ethic, and ambition.

## What is your career and what is your day to day in your line of work?

I am a realtor. I work in residential real estate, which is single-family homes, condos, townhomes, and paired homes.

Many people think it's just about selling homes for my day to day, but it isn't. I guess I was naive when I got into this business, thinking that's all it was, but a large part of real estate is marketing yourself. This is the same in many industries where if people don't know you, they can't turn to you for help. You have to get your name out there, so if they ever need help buying or selling a home, or let's say they need a contractor for some home improvement, then they know who to go to and ask. A lot of it is marketing and talking to people, networking in my business. We use Zillow lead, so we are linked with Zillow. When people are looking on Zillow for homes, they click on a house, and we receive a call. We primarily help people that are first-time homebuyers. We walk them through the process and hopefully get them to the point where they can buy their first home.

Then other people have bought a couple of homes wanting to live in different areas or need four bedrooms instead of three bedrooms, because they've had more kids, or maybe due to COVID. They are at home now, and they need an office. We will take them through their current home's selling process and help them transition to buying another house. Then others are empty nesters and want to downsize. Many are downsizing and moving out of state, while others are moving into a retirement community or transitioning ranch-style homes because they cannot use the stairs anymore. There's are people in all stages of life. I love helping people at different stages in their lives. What do they need? Do they need to buy their first home? Do they need to move up because now they got married and they have kids? Do they want to keep the house that they bought when they were a first-time homebuyer? There is so much when it comes to real estate, and it's genuinely just helping people.

It is crucial to make the process as seamless as possible with the least amount of stress. For instance, the family I am working with now, a mother and grandmother. We helped them buy a house so they can live together, and we sell the grandmother's house. It was a very stressful time. People were very stressed, especially when there's a transition that they don't want. It is vital to make the process as stress-free as possible to help them easily move on to that next chapter of their life. I intend to help people through the transition and help them be happy and move on.

Right now, I am helping someone who has been struggling with an alcohol addiction. We are in the process of getting his house ready to sell; it needed a lot of work —new carpet, new flooring, fresh paint—but really, what needs to happen is he needs to get sober. He needs to move out of his house and move in with his brother. It is interesting how real estate ties into people's lives. When he came to my office in August, I think he was reaching out for help. He was drunk. He was hiccupping the whole time. He said, 'I need to sell my house because I can't afford to make my payments anymore." I think many other real estate agents would dismiss him. But I ended up staying in touch with them; he ended up calling his brother, who lives in Texas, and gave his brother my number. The brother was glad that I have been with him since August talking to him and helping him get out of this situation. It carried several ill feelings. To move on, he needs to sell that house, cut those ties, and start a new life.

## How has COVID-19 affected your work?

When COVID started in February, we were continuing businesses as usual. We were able to show homes, meet with clients, and have open houses. Then slowly, as more restrictions came, and the virus became prevalent. There is a real estate commission that oversees each state. It is similar to the government; you have the county real estate and the state real estate commission. To show homes, you have to wear masks, wear gloves, and sanitize the house after leaving. You would meet your clients, keep your distance, and follow those regulations. Everyone has to wear masks and gloves; then we go into a home with our Clorox wipes.

After we are done showing the house, I go around and clean every surface that could have been touched by my clients or me. Honestly, that got me a bit; it took away from the experience of actually looking at the home. I would be so focused on 'what did my client touch' because some houses have cameras. I was scared because I did not want to lose my real estate license, but I wanted to continue to show homes. It became challenging to stay within compliance and get the supplies that weren't available in stores. I somehow made it through. After maintaining that procedure for a while, they stopped open houses. They just shut down real estate all together for like six weeks straight, no showing homes, no meeting clients for appointments on listing their homes, or anything. We had no work, and we couldn't do anything. This shutdown all occurred when a lot of businesses were applying for those small business loans. A lot of companies collapsed.

I was expecting many more people to be out of work and many people to be having to sell their homes due to not being able to make their mortgage payments. The mortgage industry stepped up. The banks gave people a forbearance—'the action of refraining from exercising a legal right, especially enforcing the payment of a debt' (definition provided by Oxford Languages). For example, the man I discussed earlier that is struggling with alcohol addiction applied for forbearance. The mortgage companies took whatever payments he couldn't make and tacked it to the end of his loan. Many were able to go for three months or six months without paying their mortgage, and it helped them keep their homes, so now we are not in a place where homes are being foreclosed.

But as you know, we lost a lot of business during those six weeks, but overall real estate has been very good this year, even with COVID, the shutdown, and having to wear masks and gloves. For some reason, people were still buying and selling homes. Overall t has been an excellent year for real estate. People, I think people still need to move on with their lives. They needed a COVID home where they could have like a schoolroom for their kids for online schooling, or the husband or wife needed an office. Suddenly they needed their home to have more functionalities. COVID prevented us from hosting open houses. Even today, we really can't hold open houses because they don't want a large group of people in a home at the same time. You have one family come in at a time and follow all the guidelines of staying six feet apart, wearing your mask and gloves, and sanitizing in between each showing. But at the same time, it's been an excellent year for real estate.

**So how are you able to overcome these struggles that arose from the pandemic?**

I think staying positive and making sure that I have all my supplies. Also, real estate requires a lot of paperwork. Lawyers create all of the real estate documents regarding the COVID restrictions and other paperwork. We needed our clients to sign waivers saying that they would not hold us liable, hold the homeowner responsible, or anybody accountable if they got COVID. If they are going to go out and look at a house, they needed to sign a form. The other agents would have to sign a form. Whether it's for Coldwell Banker, REMAX professionals, or with the Department of real estate, everybody had their document that required a signature.

To get through all of this is just being mindful of everything needed to maintain your license. Also, keep practicing real estate, follow the rules in place, and staying positive.

**How has your marketing or real estate strategy changed or have been influenced by the COVID-19 pandemic?**

With REMAX pros, we have client appreciation with events throughout the year. We usually hold a concert in the park and a Rockies game to invite all of our clients. We also throw a fall festival where we cook pancakes and have tethered balloon rides in a REMAX air balloon. However, all the events have been canceled this year. We will not have any client appreciation parties, and we needed to think of other ways to market, which boiled down to just talking to people and showing them that we still care. We started focusing on the little things, such as sending appreciation gifts, because we can't throw a client appreciation party.

**Could you provide an example of a specific situation that COVID impacted a project and how you were able to find a solution to overcome it?**

Well, since the beginning of February, we haven't been able to use our usual process of meeting with a client and developing a strategy to market their home. It's been the same for a while, you work with someone for like a month or two, and then they close on their home, whether they are selling it or buying it. Now it's a new process of helping people buy and sell homes during COVID. So there hasn't been one specific incident. It's just been learning how to cope with the new rules and continually adapting.

**Do you have any advice for teenagers for marketing themselves?**

There were many things that I didn't know. But let's say a younger person wanted to get involved in real estate; I would love to talk to them because I think I have many different ideas on opportunities someone could try. If you're breaking through and starting in real estate, you can look for a team that needs a showing agent. This allows you to get your feet wet and to try to get into the real estate profession. If you joined a team that needed someone to show homes, you could be the primary showing agent, as long as you're a go-getter and a self-starter. If you're a people person, it would be great to be like a showing agent.

**Do you have any advice for teenagers or young adults wanting to start in Real Estate now?**

Another way to get into real estate is through photography. We always need good photographers to take professional pictures of homes. The new thing that's come out during COVID is not just pictures of the house but also virtual tours. This is an excellent opportunity because some people wanted to see homes, but they weren't sure if that was the house they wanted to see. Many didn't want to go into every home, so if a listing had a virtual tour, they could go through the home as if they were walking through it themself.

Social media has been essential for real estate. Since you cannot go out with people and have large gatherings, having a social media person in your business is vital. If you love social media and marketing, get in with a real estate company and start that way. I think joining a team and not starting as a single agent in this day and age will help you gain a lot of experience and support.

**You discussed how important it is to stay focused and motivated, how do you keep your priorities at the forefront?**

Last year, I was a single agent but later decided to join a real estate team; this happens to be a woman-led group. There were only four members and only one male; together, we created vision boards. It was my first time making a vision board, but I enjoyed it very much. I looked at it all the time. It was great to get all of our goals, thoughts and dreams onto this vision board. Even though this terrible year of COVID, I would look back at my Vision Board and see all the goals I have accomplished. This year, I wanted to share that with everyone, so I teamed up with I Am Remarkable. We recently sent out an invite announcing our free workshop; however, it was primarily women.

When creating my Vision Board, I always put my family in the middle because everything I do revolves around my family. I also incorporated the word 'mindfulness.' In particular, mindfulness is essential because countless people don't believe in themselves. At your age, you can do anything you desire, but you have to make it happen.

**What advice would you give teenagers that are having difficulties discovering what career they would like to pursue?**

Someone who's trying to decide their career they would like to do should take time to think about what they enjoy. What do you want to do? What do you find enjoyment? Let's say you decide you're going to grab a canvas, and you're going to start painting. Well, that is one of your passions. Think about what you enjoy doing in your daily life, and then try to figure out a profession that uses your desires and hobbies. Many people think I want to do this because they believe that this specific career will make a lot of money. But really, you can be successful in your passion. You have to think about a job that fits you.

**What advice would you give someone aspiring for your career?**

People interested in Real Estate know that it's a lot of hard work and know that there's a lot of rejection. You have to know that not everybody will want to work with you, and you will not want to work with every client. You need to have a lot of people skills and be a self-starter. You work off commission; you don't get a salary. Real Estate is not having an hourly wage; you have to pay to play. I have desk fees that I have to pay REMAX professionals. If I don't make any money for three months, I still pay my desk fees for REMAX, payout myself so I may pay taxes, and pay for marketing. If you would like to do it and you have to be motivated to do it.

# TEN QUESTIONS WITH PROFESSIONAL YOGA INSTRUCTOR ERYT 20, GABRIELLA TORRES

Gabriella Torres obtained her Bachelor's Degree in Psychology and Studio Art from the University of Central Florida. Later on, she received her Master's Degree in Art, Marriage, and Family Therapy from Loyola Marymount University. After pursuing both degrees, Torres resided in Marina Del Rey, California, to further her Art, Marriage, and Family Therapy knowledge.

As a healing artist, Torres is currently based in Miami,

Florida, where she intertwines art, psychology, and yoga to create a fulfilling experience for her clients. Utilizing nature Torres began developing her unique skills to build an increasing presence of joy, peace, and tranquility in individuals' lives by prioritizing nature and healthy living. Torres believes it is incredibly vital to encourage mind, body, emotions, and spiritual well-being in everyday life.

Torres has studied and incorporated traditional medicines and healing rituals used by ancient cultures in her work in the past. Since her arrival to Miami, Florida, in 2013, she has effectively created a strategy to help people in their everyday lives by combining her interests in nature with her knowledge from her degrees. For example, Torres founded her "Vision Book," which fuses art therapy and a more in-depth version of "Vision Boarding" to deliver a unique angle to well-being, healing, life, and achieving goals.

**What is your career, and what do you do for your work?**

I am a professional yoga instructor ERYT 200, licensed marriage and family therapist, and registered art therapist. In short, I would say I am a wellness entrepreneur. I teach yoga privately and through my virtual studio, yoga retreats, and semi-private settings at the moment. My business is about health, well-being through a consistent practice of yoga and self-care tools.

## What is your philosophy in your work?

The philosophy of the work that I do is for us to live our best healthiest selves as consistently as we can. Yoga requires discipline, so practicing this discipline with ourselves and our mind, bodies, emotions, and spirit becomes a way to live a life that is healthier, fuller, and more enjoyable.

## How has COVID-19 affected your work?

We had to switch for a time to a more virtual space, in the beginning when there was not that much information available about the virus. My business became more close-knit and private than before.

## How were you able to overcome these struggles?

I minimized time in the studio and focused more on the one-to-one clients and small groups. It created an intimacy to the business that I valued very much and was a great gift from this whole scenario. My students and I became closer. That I see has a blessing.

**How have you helped your clients that have struggled mentally/emotionally during this pandemic?**

Consistency is the basic foundation through my work, as I said previously. So, because my students have become so disciplined to show up to their practice, they luckily stay more afloat and high vibe than many people. Practicing at whatever rhythm or frequency, they choose to but at least every week assisted everyone to have a healing space regularly to channel physically any anxieties or uncertainty and to create a positive outlook on the situation.

**Do you have any advice for those facing difficulties coping with separation from society?**

My advice for those who have been facing difficulties coping with separation from society is to connect. To take the time to connect to yourself, find the things that you like to do within your home, such as reading, listening to a good podcast, watching interesting films, and at-home hobbies. Then, stay connected to others by taking the time to write them, call them, FaceTime, join online workout communities, or find a way to stay connected to others. I recommend finding ways to learn to love your time by yourself and use it to further your personal development. I began to learn a new language, for example. Find ways to be productive with your time for your evolution.

**How have you been able to cope with this stressful situation?**

I have been able to cope with this situation by staying positive, staying close to my friends and family that I love dearly, and always utilizing my self-care tools. Yoga, meditation, nature walks, workouts, cooking, Vision Booking are all things that are healing to me, and I always know when to grab for one or the other.

**Can you explain your Vision Book and how people can implement this idea in their life?**

Vision Book is something that I gave birth to in graduate school. I always loved making books and collages in high school and when I was younger. I then had an idea to make collages of things I wanted to see in my life and create and manifest. I loved the process so much, and the Visions I was making were coming true. I began to share this concept with my students and therapy clients, and everybody loved and experienced things coming to life for them. I then trademarked the book series and am currently working on one for adults and children. Our mission is to create a non-profit organization to provide Vision Books every year for underprivileged children so that they can remember the magic in dreaming and living a life of their fullest potential.

**What advice would you give to teenagers that are having difficulties discovering what career they would live to pursue?**

My advice is to begin to ask yourself what you love. What excites you. If you were to forget about your family or parent's opinions, where do you find yourself? Begin to do some research. Look at different university and graduate school programs and start to hone into the things that interest you. Also, be open to changing your mind as you go. It is not always so clear to us from the beginning where we want to end up, and that is okay. Be open to learn and never deny yourself a class or workshop that interests you. Go for that.

**What advice would you give to someone aspiring for your career?**

The advice I would give to someone aspiring for my line of work is to say to go for it! If you love it, it is so rewarding. Stay consistent and stay open to finding yourself and your way within the line of work. We all have unique gifts to share with the world, and it is about finding ways to share ourselves genuinely and authentically.

# ACKNOWLEDGEMENT

I want to thank all my family and friends for all the love and assistance along the way. Ghislaine Bruner, my mother, has immensely helped me with all my projects and ideas since I was a little girl. Additionally, my father, Marc Bruner, has continually driven me to strive for success and think long-term. My little brother, Michael Bruner, who is my greatest ally and most magnificent competition, I am excited to see what you conquer in the future. I would also like to thank my little sister, Giselle Bruner, for being a ball of creativity and inspiration every day.

I want to take a moment to acknowledge and thank all of my phenomenal mentors who have helped me strive for excellence; I am abundantly grateful to have those individuals in my life. I could not be where I am today without many of my peers, especially all my writers and editors for

Ression Magazine.

Finally, I want to appreciate each of the individuals who contributed a "Ten Questions With" interview for The Leaders of Progress and Ression Magazine: J. Austin Akers, Brett Reizen, Amelia Marcum, Julio Torres, M.D., F.A.C.S., Morgan Montgomery, Ghislaine G. Torres Bruner, Esq., Ginelle Torres, Stephanie Shiver-Hogan, Leah White, Gabriella Torres, Rachel Saltzman-Friedland, Esq. and Heather Younger, Esq. I am incredibly grateful for the time and conversations we shared. All of you are inspirations, and I hope to one day follow in your footsteps, contributing to advancing progress in this world.

# ABOUT THE AUTHOR

## Juliette M. Bruner

Juliette Bruner is the Chief Executive Officer, Founder, Publisher, and Editor-in-Chief of Ression Magazine, a publication dedicated to highlighting progress in the world. Founded in May 2020, Ression is an internationally based publication with representatives from around the world and United States. The magazine targets audiences ranging from middle school through past college to promote progress in Beauty, Politics, Entertainment, Study, Wellness, Business, and Sports. Ression Magazine's goal is to inspire the next generation of leaders to continue progress in the world. You can Subscribe to Ression Magazine at https://ressionmagazine.com or follow us on Twitter, Instagram, or FaceBook @ressionmagazine.

Bruner is currently a senior at Regis Jesuit High School located in Colorado, and aspires to follow in the footsteps of Ruth Bader Ginsburg, Michelle Obama, Colin Powell, Tulsi Gabbard, Missy Franklin (Regis Jesuit '13), Elon Musk, and all of the those interviewed for The Leaders of Progress.

Made in the USA
Monee, IL
31 March 2021